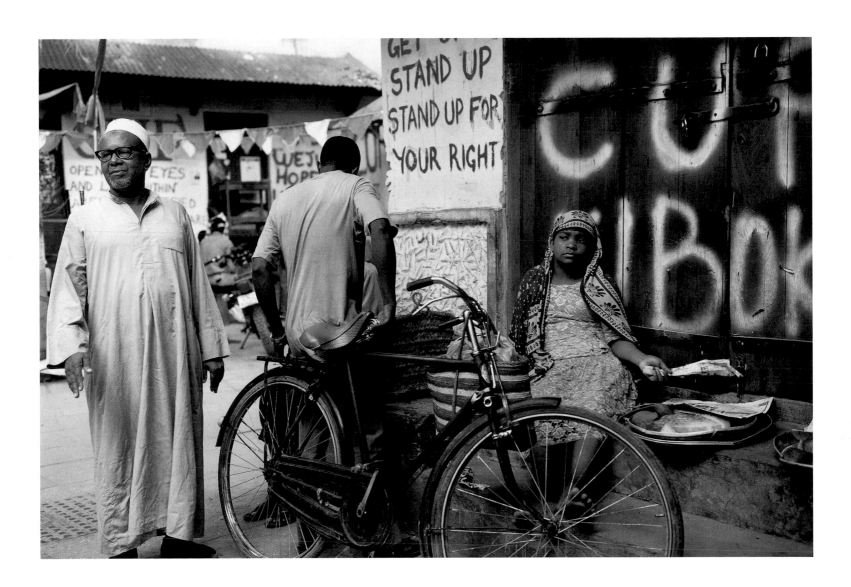

Photographs by Robert Lyons

Essay and Poems by Chinua Achebe

Another Africa

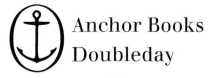

Anchor Books
Doubleday

New York London Toronto Sydney Auckland

A Mother in a Refugee Camp

No Madonna and Child could touch
Her tenderness for a son
She soon would have to forget. . . .
The air was heavy with odors of diarrhea,
Of unwashed children with washed-out ribs
And dried-up bottoms waddling in labored steps
Behind blown empty bellies. Other mothers there
Had long ceased to care, but not this one:
She held a ghost-smile between her teeth,
And in her eyes the memory
Of a mother's pride. . . . She had bathed him
And rubbed him down with bare palms.
She took from their bundle of possessions
A broken comb and combed
The rust-colored hair left on his skull
And then—humming in her eyes—began to part it.
In their former life this was perhaps
A little daily act of no consequence
Before his breakfast and school; now she did it
Like putting flowers on a tiny grave.

18

Knowing Robs Us

Knowing robs us of wonder.
Had it not ripped apart
the fearful robes of primordial Night
to steal the force that crafted horns
on doghead and sowed insurrection
overnight in the homely beak
of a hen; had reason not given us
assurance that day will daily break
and the sun's array return to disarm
night's fantastic figurations—
each daybreak
would be garlanded at the city gate
and escorted with royal drums
to a stupendous festival
of an amazed world.

One day
after the passage of a dark April storm
ecstatic birds followed its furrows
sowing songs of daybreak though the time
was now past noon, their sparkling
notes sprouting green incantations
everywhere to free the world
from harmattan death.

But for me
the celebration is make-believe;
the clamorous change of season
will darken the hills of Nsukka
for an hour or two when it comes;
no hurricane will hit my sky—
and no song of deliverance.

26

Agostinho Neto

Neto, were you no more
Than the middle one favored by fortune
In children's riddle; Kwame
Striding ahead to accost
Demons; behind you a laggard third
As yet unnamed, of twisted fingers?

No! Your secure strides
Were hard earned. Your feet
Learned their fierce balance
In violent slopes of humiliation;
Your delicate hands, patiently
Groomed for finest incisions,
Were commandeered brusquely to kill,
Your melodious voice to battle-cry.

Perhaps your family and friends
Knew a merry flash cracking the gloom
We see in pictures but I prefer
And will keep that sorrowful legend.
For I have seen how
Half a millennium of alien rape
And murder can stamp a smile
On the vacant face of the fool,
The sinister grin of Africa's idiot-kings
Who oversee in obscene palaces of gold
The butchery of their own people.

Neto, I sing your passing, I,
Timid requisitioner of your vast
Armory's most congenial supply.
What shall I sing? A dirge answering
The gloom? No, I will sing tearful songs
Of joy; I will celebrate
The Man who rode a trinity
Of awesome fates to the cause
Of our trampled race!
Thou Healer, Soldier and Poet!

41

47

A Wake for Okigbo

For whom are we searching?
For whom are we searching?
For Okigbo we are searching!

          Nzomalizo!

Has he gone for firewood, let him return.
Has he gone to fetch water, let him return.
Has he gone to the marketplace, let him return.
For Okigbo we are searching.

          Nzomalizo!

For whom are we searching?
For whom are we searching?
For Okigbo we are searching?

          Nzomalizo!

Has he gone for firewood, may Ugboko not take him.
Has he gone to the stream, may Iyi not swallow him!
Has he gone to the market, then keep from him you
    Tumult of the marketplace!
Has he gone to battle,
    please Ogbonuke step aside for him!
For Okigbo we are searching!

          Nzomalizo!

They bring home a dance, who is to dance it for us?
They bring home a war, who will fight it for us?
The one we call repeatedly,
    there's something he alone can do
It is Okigbo we are calling!

          Nzomalizo!

Witness the dance, how it arrives
The war, how it has broken out
But the caller of the dance is nowhere to be found
The brave one in battle is nowhere in sight!
Do you not see now that whom we call again
And again, there is something he alone can do?
It is Okigbo we are calling!

          Nzomalizo!

The dance ends abruptly
The spirit dancers fold their dance and depart in midday
Rain soaks the stalwart, soaks the two-sided drum!
The flute is broken that elevates the spirit
The music pot shattered that accompanies the leg in
    its measure
Brave one of my blood!
Brave one of Igbo land!
Brave one in the middle of so much blood!
Owner of riches in the dwelling place of spirit
Okigbo is the one for whom I am searching!

          Nzomalizo!

Translated from the Igbo by Ifeanyi Menkiti

51

54

Butterfly

Speed is violence
Power is violence
Weight violence

The butterfly seeks safety in lightness
In weightless, undulating flight

But at a crossroads where mottled light
From trees falls on a brash new highway
Our convergent territories meet

I come power-packed enough for two
And the gentle butterfly offers
Itself in bright yellow sacrifice
Upon my hard silicon shield.

64

69

74

The Nigerian Chief and the Census

I will not mourn with you
your lost populations, the silent columns
of your fief erased
from the king's book of numbers

For in your house of stone
by the great road
you listened once to refugee voices
at dawn telling of massacres and plagues
in their land across seven rivers

Like a hornbill in flight
you tucked in your slippered feet
from the threshold
out of their beseeching gaze

But pestilence farther
than faraway tales of dawn
had bought a seat in Ogun's reckless
chariot and knocks by nightfall
on your iron gate.

Take heart oh chief; decimation
by miscount, however grievous,
is a happy retreat from bolder uses
of the past. Take heart,
for these scribal flourishes
behind smudged entries, these
trophied returns of clerical headhunters
can never match the quiet flow
of red blood.

But if my grudging comfort fail,
then take this long and even view to AD 2000
when the word is due to go out again
and—depending on which Caesar
orders the count—new conurbations
may sprout in today's wastelands,
and thriving cities dissolve
in sudden mirages

and the ready-reckoners at court
will calculate their gain
and our loss, and make us
any-number-of-million-they-like strong!

84

Flying

Something in altitude kindles power-thirst
Mere horse-height suffices the emir
Bestowing from rich folds of prodigious turban
Upon crawling peasants in the dust
Rare imperceptible nods enwrapped
In princely boredom.

I too have known
A parching of that primordial palate,
A quickening to manifest life
Of a long recessive appetite.
Though strapped and manacled
That day I commanded from the pinnacle
Of a three-tiered world a bridge befitting
The proud deranged deity I had become.
A magic rug of rushing clouds
Billowed out its white softnesses
Like practised *houri* fingers on my sole
And through filters of its gauzy fabric
Revealed wonders of a metropolis
Magic-struck to fairyland proportions.
By different adjustments of vision
I caused the clouds to float
Over a stilled landscape, over towers
And masts and smoke-plumed chimneys;
Or turned the very earth, unleashed
From itself, a roaming fugitive
Beneath a constant sky. Then came

A sudden brightness over the world,
A rare winter's smile it was, and printed
On my cloud carpet a black cross
Set in an orb of rainbows. To which
Splendid nativity came—who else would come
But grey unsporting Reason, faithless
Pedant offering a bald refractory annunciation?
But oh what beauty! what speed!
A phantom chariot in panic flight
From Our Royal Proclamation of the rites
Of day! And riding out our procession
Of phantasy we slaked an ancient
Vestigial greed shrivelled by ages of dormancy
Till the eyes exhausted by glorious pageantries
Returned and rested on that puny
Legend of the life-jacket stowed away
Under my seat, of all places.
Now I think I know why gods
Are so partial to heights—to mountain
Tops and spires, to proud *iroko* trees
And thorn-guarded holy bombax,
Why petty household divinities
Will sooner perch on a rude board
Strung precariously from brittle rafters
Of a thatched roof than sit squarely
On safe earth.

94

96

100

Africa's Tarnished Name

IT IS A GREAT IRONY OF HISTORY and geography that Africa, whose land mass is closer than any other to the mainland of Europe, should come to occupy in European psychological disposition the farthest point of otherness, should indeed become Europe's very antithesis. The French-African poet and statesman Leopold Sedar Senghor, in full awareness of this paradox, chose to celebrate that problematic proximity in a poem, "Prayer to Masks," with the startling imagery of one of nature's most profound instances of closeness: "joined together at the navel." And why not? After all, the shores of northern Africa and southern Europe enclose, like two cupped hands, the waters of the world's most famous sea, perceived by the ancients as the very heart and center of the world. Senghor's metaphor would have been better appreciated in the days of ancient Egypt and Greece than today.

History aside, geography has its own kind of lesson in paradox for us. This lesson, which was probably lost on everyone else except those of us living in West Africa in the last days of the British Raj, was the ridiculous fact of longitudinal equality between London, mighty imperial metropolis, and Accra, rude rebel camp of colonial insurrection—so that, their unequal stations in life notwithstanding, they were bisected by the same Greenwich meridian and thus doomed together to the same time of day!

But longitude is not all there is in life. There is also latitude, which gives London and Accra very different experiences of midday temperature, for example, and perhaps gave their inhabitants over past eons of time radically different complexions. So differences are there, if those are what one is looking for. But there is no way in which such differences as do exist could satisfactorily explain the profound perception of alienness that Africa has come to represent for Europe.

This perception problem is not in its origin a result of ignorance, as we are sometimes inclined to think. At least it is not ignorance entirely, or even primarily. It was in general a deliberate *invention* devised to facilitate two gigantic, historical events: the Atlantic slave trade and the colonization of Africa by Europe, the second event following closely on the heels of the first, and the two together stretching across almost half a millennium from about

A.D. 1500. In an important and authoritative study of this invention, two American scholars, Dorothy Hammond and Alta Jablow, show how the content of British writing about Africa changed dramatically at the height of the slave trade in the eighteenth century and

> . . . shifted from almost indifferent and matter-of-fact reports of what the voyagers had seen to judgmental evaluation of the Africans. . . . The shift to such pejorative comment was due in large measure to the effects of the slave trade. A vested interest in the slave trade produced a literature of devaluation, and since the slave trade was under attack, the most derogatory writing about Africa came from its literary defenders. Dalzel, for instance, prefaced his work with an apologia for slavery: "Whatever evils the slave trade may be attended with . . . it is mercy . . . to poor wretches, who . . . would otherwise suffer from the butcher's knife." Numerous proslavery tracts appeared, all intent upon showing the immorality and degradation of Africans. . . . Enslavement of such a degraded people was thus not only justifiable but even desirable. The character of Africans could change only for the better through contact with their European masters. Slavery, in effect, became the means of the Africans' salvation, for it introduced them to Christianity and civilization.[1]

The vast arsenal of derogatory images of Africa amassed to defend the slave trade and, later, colonization, gave the world not only a literary tradition that is now, happily, defunct, but also a particular way of looking (or rather *not* looking) at Africa and Africans that endures, alas, into our own day. And so, although those sensational "African" novels that were so popular in the nineteenth century and early part of the twentieth have trickled to a virtual stop, their centuries-old obsession with lurid and degrading stereotypes of Africa has been bequeathed to the cinema, to journalism, to certain varieties of anthropology, even to humanitarianism and missionary work itself.

About two years ago, I saw an extraordinary program on television about the children of the major Nazi war criminals whose lives had been devastated by the burden of the guilt of their fathers. I felt quite sorry for them. And then, out of nowhere, came the information that one of them had gone into the Church and would go as a missionary to the Congo.

"What has the Congo got to do with it?" I asked of my television screen. Then I remembered the motley parade of adventurers, of saints and sinners from Europe that had been drawn to that region since it was first discovered by Europe in 1482—Franciscan monks, Jesuit priests, envoys from the kings of Portugal, agents of King Leopold of the Belgians, H. M. Stanley, Roger Casement, Joseph Conrad, Albert Schweitzer, ivory hunters and rubber merchants, slave traders, explorers. They all made their visit and left their mark for good or ill. And the Congo, like the ancient tree by the much-used farm road, bears on its bark countless scars of the machete.

A saint like Schweitzer can give one a lot more trouble than King Leopold II, a villain of unmitigated guilt, because along with doing good and saving African lives, Schweitzer also managed to say that the African was indeed his brother, but only his *junior* brother.

But of all the hundreds and thousands of European visitors to the Congo region in the last five hundred years, there was perhaps no other with the deftness and sleight-of-hand of Joseph Conrad or the depth of the wound he gave that roadside tree. In his Congo novella, *Heart of Darkness*, Conrad managed to transform elements from centuries of generally crude and fanciful writing about Africans into a piece of "serious" literature.

Halfway through his story, Conrad describes a journey up the River Congo in the 1890s as though it were the very first encounter between conscious humanity coming from Europe and an unconscious, primeval hegemony that had apparently gone nowhere since the world was created. Naturally, it is the conscious party that tells the story:

> We were wanderers on a prehistoric earth, on the earth that wore
> the aspect of an unknown planet. We could have fancied

ourselves the first of men taking possession of an accursed inheritance.[2]

Prehistoric earth . . . unknown planet . . . fancied ourselves . . . the first of men . . . This passage, which is Conrad at his best, or his worst, according to the reader's predilection, goes on at some length through *a burst of yells, a whirl of black limbs,* of *hands clapping, feet stamping, bodies swaying, eyes rolling,* through *a black incomprehensible frenzy* to *the prehistoric man* himself, *in the night of first ages.* And then Conrad delivers his famous coup de grâce. Were these prehistoric creatures really human? And he answers the question with the most sophisticated ambivalence of double negatives:

> No they were not inhuman. Well, you know that was the worst of it—this suspicion of their not being inhuman.[3]

Perhaps this is a good point for me to anticipate the kind of objection some people expressed when I first spoke about Conrad and *Heart of Darkness* in 1975. It was not my intention then or now to spend the rest of my life in Conrad controversy, and so I have generally kept away from both critics and defenders of my 1975 argument. But my present purpose requires that I take up one particular line of objection, one which presumes to teach me how to distinguish a book of fiction from, say, a book of history or sociology. My critics do not put it as brutally as that; they are very kind. One of them actually took the trouble to write a letter to me and offer his good offices to reconcile me with Conrad because, as he said, Conrad was actually *on my side!* I did not, however, take up this kind mediation offer because I was not talking about *sides.* For me there is only one, *human,* side. Full stop!

But to return to Conrad and the word *fancy,* which his genius had lit upon:

> We could have fancied ourselves the first of men taking possession of an accursed inheritance.

I suggest that *fancied* is the alarm-word insinuated into Conrad's dangerously highfalutin account by his genius, as well as by reason and sanity, but almost immediately crowded out, alas, by the emotional and psychological fascination he had for the long-established and well-heeled tradition of writing about Africa. Conrad was at once prisoner of this tradition and one of its most influential purveyors; he more than anyone else secured its admission into the hall of fame of "canonical" literature. Fancy, sometimes called Imagination, is not inimical to Fiction. On the contrary, they are bosom friends. But they observe a certain protocol around each other's property and around the homestead of their droll and difficult neighbor, Fact.

Conrad was a writer who kept much of his fiction fairly close to the facts of his life as a sailor. He had no obligation to do so, but that was what he chose to do—to write about places that actually exist and about people who live in them. He confessed in his 1917 "Author's Note" that

> *Heart of Darkness* is experience too, but it is experience pushed a
> little (and only very little) beyond the actual facts of the case for
> the perfectly legitimate, I believe, purpose of bringing it home to
> the minds and bosoms of the readers.[4]

One fact of the case about the River Congo which Conrad may not have known was how much traffic it had seen before it saw Conrad in the 1890s. Even if one discounts the Africans who lived on its banks and would presumably have sailed up and down it through the millennia before Conrad, there was even a European sailing ship on the Congo four hundred years before our man made his journey and wrote his book. Yes, four hundred!

The Portuguese captain Diogo Cao, who discovered the river for Europe in 1482, was actually looking for something else when he stumbled on it; he was looking for a passage around Africa into the Indian Ocean. On his second voyage he went further up the river and heard from the inhabitants of the area about a powerful ruler whose capital was still further up. Cao left four Franciscan monks to study the situation and resumed the primary purpose of his expedition. On his way back he once more detoured into the Congo to pick up his monks; but they were gone! He seized in retaliation a number of African hostages, carried them off to Lisbon, and delivered them to King Manuel of Portugal.[5] This unpropitious beginning of Europe's adventure in the heart of Africa was quickly mended when Cao returned to the Congo for the third time in 1487, bringing back his African hostages who had meanwhile learned the Portuguese language and Christian religion. Cao was taken to see the king, Mweni-Congo, seated on an ivory throne surrounded by his courtiers. Cao's monks were returned to him, and all was well.

An extraordinary period ensued in which the king of Congo became a Christian with the title of King Afonso I. Before very long,

> the royal brothers of Portugal and Congo were writing letters to each other that were couched in terms of complete equality of status. Emissaries went back and forth between them. Relations were established between Mbanza[6] and the Vatican. A son of the Mweni-Congo was appointed in Rome itself as bishop of his country.[7]

This bishop, Dom Henrique, had studied in Lisbon, and when he led a delegation of Congo noblemen to Rome for his consecration, he had addressed the Pope in Latin.

Nzinga Mbemba, baptized as Dom Afonso, was a truly extraordinary man. He learned in middle life to read and speak Portuguese, and it was said that when he examined the legal code of Portugal he was surprised by its excessive harshness. He asked the Portuguese envoy what the penalty was in his country for a citizen who dared to put his feet on the ground! This criticism was probably reported back to the king of Portugal, for in a 1511 letter to his "royal brother," Dom Afonso, he made defensive reference to differing notions of severity between the two nations.[8] Can we today imagine a situation in which an African ruler is giving, rather than receiving, admonition on law and civilization?

The Christian kingdom of Dom Afonso I in Congo did not fare well and was finally destroyed two centuries later after a long struggle with the Portuguese. The source of the problem was the determination of the Portuguese to take out of Congo as many slaves as their vast new colony in Brazil demanded, and the Congo kings' desire to limit or end the traffic. There was also a dispute over mining rights. In the war that finally ended the independence of the kingdom of Congo and established Portuguese control over it, the armies of both nations marched under Christian banners. But that is another story, for another time.

Even the sketchiest telling of this story such as I have done here still reads like a fairy tale, not because it did not happen but because we have become all too familiar with the Africa of Conrad's *Heart of Darkness,* its predecessors going back to the sixteenth century and its successors today in print and electronic media. This tradition has invented an Africa where nothing good happens or ever happened, an Africa that has not been discovered yet and is waiting for the first European visitor to explore it and explain it and straighten it up.

In Conrad's boyhood, explorers were the equivalent of today's Hollywood superstars. As a child of nine, Conrad pointed at the center of Africa on a map and said: *When I grow up I shall go there!* Among his heroes were Mungo Park, who drowned exploring the River Niger; David Livingstone, who died looking for the source of the Nile; and Dr. Barth, the first white man to approach the gates of the walled city of Kano. Conrad tells a memorable story of Barth "approaching Kano which no European eye had seen till then," and an excited population of Africans streaming out of the gates "to behold the wonder."

And Conrad also tells us how much better he liked Dr. Barth's "first-white-man" story than the story of Sir Hugh Clifford, British governor of Nigeria, traveling in state to open a college in Kano forty years later. Even though Conrad and Hugh Clifford were friends, the story and pictures of this second Kano event left Conrad "without any particular elation. Education is a great thing, but Doctor Barth gets in the way."[9]

That is neatly and honestly put. Africa of colleges is of little interest to avid lovers of unexplored Africa. In one of his last essays, Conrad describes the explorers he admired as "fathers of militant geography" or "the blessed of militant geography." Too late on the scene himself to join their ranks, did he become merely an adept conjurer of militant geography and history?

It is not a crime to prefer the Africa of explorers to the Africa of colleges. There have been some good people who did. When I was a young radio producer in Lagos in the early 1960s, a legendary figure from the first decade of British colonial rule in Nigeria returned for a final visit in her eighties. Sylvia Leith-Ross had made a very important study of Igbo women in her pioneering work *African Women*, [10] in which she established from masses of personal interviews of Igbo women that they did not fit European stereotypes of downtrodden slaves and beasts of burden. [11] She graciously agreed to do a radio program for me about Nigeria at the turn of the century. It was a wonderful program. What has stuck to my mind was when she conceded the many good, new things in the country, like Ibadan University College, and asked wistfully: "But where is my beloved bush?"

Was this the same hankering for the exotic which lay behind Conrad's preference for a lone European explorer over African education? I could hear a difference in tone. Sylvia Leith-Ross was gentle, almost self-mocking in her choice, and without the slightest hint of hostility. At worst, you might call her a starry-eyed conservationist!

Conrad is different. At best you are uncertain about the meaning of his choice. That is, until you encounter his portrait, in *Heart of Darkness*, of an African who has received the rudiments of education:

> And between whiles I had to look after the savage who was fireman. He was an improved specimen; he could fire up a vertical boiler. He was there below me and, upon my word, to look at him was as edifying as seeing a dog in a parody of breeches and a feather hat walking on his hind legs. A few months of training had done for that really fine chap. He squinted at the steam-gauge and at the water-gauge with an evident effort of intrepidity—and he had filed teeth too, the poor devil, and the wool of his pate shaved into queer patterns, and three ornamental scars on each of his

cheeks. He ought to have been clapping his hands and stamping
his feet on the bank, instead of which he was hard at work, a
thrall to strange witchcraft, full of improving knowledge.[12]

This is poisonous writing and in full consonance with the tenets of the
slave trade–inspired tradition of European portrayal of Africa. There are
endless variations in that tradition of the "problem" of education for Africa;
for example, a highly educated African might be shown sloughing off his
veneer of civilization along with his Oxford blazer when the tom-tom
begins to beat. The moral: Africa and education do not mix. Or: Africa will
revert to type.

And what is this type? Something dark and ominous and alien. At the
center of all the problems Europe has had in its perception of Africa lies
the simple question of African humanity: *Are they or are they not? Are they
truly like us?*

Conrad devised a simple hierarchical order of souls for the characters
in *Heart of Darkness.* At the bottom are the Africans whom he calls "rudi-
mentary souls." Above them are the European ivory traders—petty, vicious,
morally obtuse; he calls them "tainted souls" or "small souls." At the top are
regular Europeans, and they don't seem to have the need for an adjective.
The gauge for measuring a soul turns out to be the evil character, Mr. Kurtz,
himself; how he affects that particular soul.

He had the power to charm or frighten rudimentary souls into an
aggravated witch-dance in his honor, he could also fill the small
souls of the pilgrims with bitter misgivings—he had one devoted
friend at least and he had conquered one soul in the world that
was neither rudimentary nor tainted with self-seeking.[15]

The tendency of Africans to offer worship to any European who comes
along is another recurrent theme in European writing about Africa. Varia-
tions on it include the veneration of an empty Coca-Cola bottle that falls out
of an airplane. Even children's stories are not spared this insult, as I once

learned from foolishly buying an expensive colorful book for my little girl without first checking it out.

The aggravated witch-dance for a mad white man by hordes of African natives may accord with the needs and desires of the fabulists of the Africa that never was, but the experience of Congo was different. Far from falling over themselves to worship their invaders, the people of this region of Africa have a long history of resistance to European control. In 1687 an Italian priest, Father Cavazzi, complained:

> These nations think themselves the foremost men in the world.
> They imagine that Africa is not only the greatest part of the world,
> but also the happiest and most agreeable. . . . [Their King] is per-
> suaded that there is no other monarch in the world who is his
> equal.[14]

Between Father Cavazzi's words and Joseph Conrad's images of gyrating and babbling savages there was indeed a hiatus of two harsh centuries. Did the people of the Congo region deteriorate beyond recognition in this period and lose even the art of being human? No, they remained human through it all, to this day. I know some of them.

People are wrong when they tell you that Conrad was on the side of the Africans because his story showed great compassion toward them. Africans are not really interested in compassion, whatever it means; they ask for one thing alone—to be seen for what they are: human beings. Conrad does not grant them this favor in *Heart of Darkness.* Apparently some people can read it without seeing any problem. We simply have to be patient. But a word may be in order for the last-ditch defenders who fall back on the excuse that the racial insensitivity of Conrad was normal in his time. Even if that were so, it would still be a flaw in a serious writer—a flaw that responsible criticism today could not gloss over. But it is not even true that everybody in Conrad's day was like him. David Livingstone, an older contemporary, and by no means a saint, was different. Ironically he was also Conrad's great hero, whom he placed among the blessed of militant geography . . . a notable European figure and the most venerated perhaps of all the objects of my early geographical enthusiasm.[15]

And yet his hero's wise, inclusive humanity eluded Conrad. What did he think of Livingstone's famous judgment of Africans?

> I have found it difficult to come to a conclusion on their [African] character. They sometimes perform actions remarkably good, and sometimes as strangely the opposite. . . . After long observation, I came to the conclusion that they are just a strange mixture of good and evil as men are everywhere else.[16]

Joseph Conrad was forty-four years *younger* than David Livingstone. If his times were responsible for his racial attitude we should expect him to be more advanced than Livingstone, not more backward. Without doubt the times in which we live influence our behavior, but the best, or merely the better, among us, like Livingstone, are never held hostage by their times.

An interesting analogy may be drawn here with the visual arts imagery of Africans in eighteenth-century Britain. In 1997, an exhibition was held by the National Portrait Gallery in London on the subject of Ignatius Sancho, an African man of letters, and his contemporaries. The centerpiece of the exhibition was the famous painting of Ignatius Sancho by Thomas Gainsborough in 1768. Reyahn King describes the painting in these words:

> Gainsborough's skill is clearest in his treatment of Sancho's skin colour. Unlike Hogarth, whose use of violet pigments when painting black faces results in a greyish skin tone, the brick-red of Sancho's waistcoat in Gainsborough's portrait, combined with the rich brown background and Sancho's own skin colour make the painting unusually warm in tone as well as feeling. Gainsborough has painted thinly over a reddish base with shading in a chocolate tone and minimal colder lights on Sancho's nose, chin and lips.

The resulting face seems to glow and contrasts strongly with the vanishing effect so often suffered by the faces of black servants in the shadows of 18th-century portraits of their masters.[17]

Evidently Gainsborough put care and respect into his painting; and he produced a magnificent portrait of an African who had been born on a slave ship and, at the time of his sitting, was still a servant in an aristocratic household. But neither of these facts was allowed to take away from him his human dignity in Gainsborough's portrait.

There were other portraits of Africans in Britain painted at the same time. One of them provides a study in contrast with Gainsborough's rendering of Ignatius Sancho. The African portrayed in this other picture was one Francis Williams, a graduate of Cambridge, a poet and founder of a school in Jamaica; an amazing phenomenon in those days.[18] A portrait of him by an anonymous artist shows a man with a big, flat face lacking any distinctiveness, standing in a cluttered library on tiny broomstick legs. It was clearly an exercise in mockery. Perhaps Francis Williams aroused resentment because of his rare accomplishments. Certainly the anonymous scarecrow portrait was intended to put him in his place in much the same way as the philosopher, David Hume, was said to have dismissed Williams's accomplishments and compared the admiration people had for him to the praise they might give "a parrot who speaks a few words plainly."

It is clear, then, that in eighteenth-century Britain there were Britons like the painter Gainsborough who were ready to accord respect to an African, even an African who was a servant; and there were other Britons like the anonymous painter of Francis Williams, or the eminent philosopher, Hume, who would sneer at a black man's achievement. And it was not so much a question of the times in which they lived as the kind of people they were. It was the same in the times of Joseph Conrad a century later, and it is the same today!

Things have not gone well in Africa for quite a while. The era of colonial freedom that began so optimistically with Ghana in 1957 would soon be captured by Cold War manipulators and skewed into a deadly season of ostensible ideological conflicts, encouraging the emergence of all kinds of evil rulers able to count on limitless supplies of military hardware from their overseas patrons, no matter how atrociously they ruled their peoples.

With the sudden end of the Cold War, these rulers or their successor regimes have lost their value to their sponsors and have been cast on the rubbish heap and forgotten, along with their nations.

Disaster parades today with impunity through the length and breadth of much of Africa: war, genocide, dictatorship, military government, corruption, collapsed economy, poverty, disease, and every ill attendant upon political and social chaos!

It is necessary for these sad conditions to be reported because evil thrives best in quiet, untidy corners. In many African countries, however, the local news media cannot report these events without unleashing serious and sometimes fatal consequences. And so the foreign correspondent is frequently the only means of getting an important story told, or of drawing the world's attention to disasters in the making or being covered up. Such an important role is risky in more ways than one. It can expose the correspondent to actual physical danger; but there is also the moral danger of colonizing another's story. This will immediately raise the question of the character and attitude of the correspondent. For the same qualities of mind that separated a Conrad from a Livingstone, or a Gainsborough and an anonymous painter of Francis Williams, are still present and active today. Perhaps this difference can best be put in one phrase: the presence or absence of respect for the human person.

In a 1997 calendar issued by Amnesty International USA jointly with the International Center of Photography, a brief but important editorial message criticizes some current journalistic practices:

> The apocalyptic vision of the newsmakers [does not] accurately
> document the world community. Nor are they particularly helpful
> in forming a picture of our common humanity.[19]

And it goes on to set down the principles that guided its own selection of twelve photographs in the calendar as follows:

> [They] document an authentic humanity. They also communicate the fact that every person, everywhere, possesses an inalienable rightness and an imperishable dignity—two qualities that must be respected and protected."[20]

Robert Lyons's photographs of Africa seem to me to possess these qualities of respect. I wish I could say the same of a documentary film that I have seen twice in the last three years or so on PBS. It was about sex and reproduction through the entire gamut of living things, from the simplest single-cell creatures in the water to complex organisms like fishes and birds and mammals. It was a very skillful scientific program that pulled no punches when it came to where babies came from. It was all there in its starkness. Was it necessary to conclude this graphic reproductive odyssey with man (or rather woman)? I did not think so. The point (whatever it was) had already been made with apes, including, I believe, those that invented the "missionary position."

But the producers of the documentary were quite uncompromising in their exhaustiveness. And so a woman in labor *was* exposed to show the baby coming out of her. But the real shock was that everybody in that labor room was white except the Ghanaian (by her accent) mother in childbirth. Why were all the rest white? Because it was all happening in a hospital in London, not in Accra.

I am sure that the producers of that program would reject with indignation any suggestion that their choice of candidate was influenced in any way by race. And they might even be right, in the sense that they would not have had a meeting of their production team to decide that a white woman would not be an appropriate subject. But the fact is that such deliberation would not be necessary today, except perhaps in the crude caucuses of the lunatic fringe. Race is no longer a visible member of the boardroom. That much progress must be conceded; and it is not to be sniffed at. But an invisible member with a vote is still a deadly threat to justice. The lesson for that production team, and for the rest of us, is that when we are comfortable and inattentive, we run the risk of committing grave injustices absentmindedly.

—Chinua Achebe
January 20, 1998

NOTES

1. *The Africa That Never Was: Four Centuries of British Writing about Africa* (Prospect Heights: Waveland Press, 1992), pp. 22–23.

2. *Heart of Darkness,* ed. Robert Kimbrough (New York: W. W. Norton), p. 37.

3. Ibid.

4. Ibid., p. 4.

5. I am indebted to Basil Davidson's *The African Slave Trade* (Boston: Little, Brown and Company, 1980) for the outline of this story.

6. The capital of the kingdom of Congo, which the king soon renamed San Salvador.

7. Davidson, p. 156.

8. Ibid., p. 152.

9. Ibid., p. 147.

10. *African Women: A Study of the Ibo of Nigeria* (London: Faber & Faber, 1938).

11. Ibid., p. 19.

12. Conrad, pp. 38–39.

13. Ibid., p. 51.

14. Davidson, p. 29.

15. Conrad, p. 147.

16. *Missionary Travels*, quoted by Hammond and Jablow, p. 43.

17. King, Reyahn, et al., *Ignatius Sancho: An African Man of Letters* (London: National Portrait Gallery, 1997), p. 28.

18. Ibid., p. 30.

19. Schulz, William F., and Willis Hartshorn, *1997 Amnesty International: Photographs from the Collection of the International Center of Photography* (New York: Universe Publishing), p. 1.

20. Ibid.

Photographer's Note

I WAS AND STILL AM AN OUTSIDER TO AFRICA. I am a foreigner who brings my own preferences, biases, and tastes to what I see. It is this outsider perspective that is at the core of this book. Through the process of returning time and again to Africa, my perspective has evolved. Coupled with a practiced naïveté, this perspective has allowed me to enter situations often unnerving or uncomfortable to peer into, and create imagery that is simultaneously from within and without. I continually choose *that moment, that light, that gesture,* and *that framing* to construct the image. It is difficult to put into words what the sum of these idiosyncratic choices is, except to say that, taken together, they present a specific style of seeing.

I gave this book its title, "Another Africa," in part to counteract the constant portrayal of Africa as a place beset by famine, drought, and civil war, or as an open-air ethnographic museum for the West. It would be presumptuous to think that the images in this book could define the place. Africa is a vast and complex continent, whose name conjures in one's mind a myriad of imagery and mythology. It is a place of incredible richness embroidered by traditions at play in modern times.

I have kept journals of my travels throughout the past nine years. Sometimes I've only noted names and addresses of individuals to whom I wish to send or bring back photographs; at other times, views of a particular time and place. The following excerpts convey some of my experiences.

SUDAN 1989–90   "Arrived by steamer to Wadi Halfa . . . spent a few hours hanging out waiting for transport south, a lorry finally pulls up. It has about thirty or so people already on board, sheep, and luggage. . . . The sun is quite amazing as it sets on the desert landscape, grand mounds of black stone and red sand, mixing with the blue, cyan, and magenta sunset. . . ."

KHARTOUM 1989–90   ". . . uncertainty, apathy, curfews, permits, bureaucracy, petrol lines, sugar shortages, bread shortages, refugees from Erítrea, Ethiopia, and elsewhere. Riding the bus Christmas Eve with Mohammed, a former Olympic contestant, at the wheel, he tells me things are difficult at the moment, then he laughs a deep laugh and takes out a canteen filled with homemade brew, about 150 proof. . . . Sharia law has been imposed since June, to be caught with alcohol is a grave offense, but it's Christmas Eve, a time to celebrate, the curfew was lifted only hours ago to allow Christians [Southern Sudanese] to attend midnight mass. . . ."

BAMAKO 1991 "Arrived last night, lots of dust, an empty dreary airport. There were seven or eight taxis waiting to take visitors downtown, about thirty minutes away. Lights are visible through haze and dust. We had to push the taxi to get it started. . . . Awoke this morning to the sound of hundreds of voices chanting, then windows breaking . . . it seems I have arrived at an important time."

MALI 1995 "The trip in Dogon has been quite incredible, not only for what I saw, but for what I did not see. I did not see the material luxuries that distinguish and isolate people from each other in the West. I did not see TVs, stores, buses, telephones, faddish fashion; in fact, the harshness of the environment bred a kind of equality among all the people, except of course visiting Westerners, who always know it is only for a short period that they are here without the 'comforts' of home."

KENYA 1996 "Kakuma to Lokichokio to Labune to Warus—I am not sure really what to expect or even how far I will get—I can only hope to actually get into Sudan—how shall I call it, the New Sudan, the Southern Sudan? Of course there is always the possibility I will not get in again at all, but I will have tried, and, after all, it is the journey, not the destination, that is really the aim."

—Robert Lyons
  Seattle, 1998

Titles

Acknowledgments

This project could not have been realized without the support and help of numerous individuals.

First, I would like to thank the following people for their assistance in Africa: Gideon Taylor of the AJDC in Ethiopia, Sally Burnheim of Operation Lifeline Sudan, Fatuma Juma and Sankei Ketan of Radda Barnen, and Ray Victurine and Sarah Tifft in Uganda. A special thanks to Mamadou Traore and Abdel Kader M'boup for their help and friendship.

For their assistance in retrieving my original negatives from a studio fire in 1996, I shall always be indebted to Andrew Firth, Lauren Traub, Marco Prozzo, and Andrea Auge. A very special thanks to Chiyo Ishikawa, who throughout the aftermath of the fire was always there for me in ways I cannot begin to describe.

I wish to acknowledge the generous assistance of Gary Magruder, Fuji Photo Film USA Inc., Byron Davalos and Durst ACS Inc., and all the people at Glazer's Photographic Supply.

Many of these photographs were printed in collaboration with my assistant, Andrew Firth, whose skills were indispensable to me. He has given much enthusiasm, energy, and patience to this project and has been invaluable in all phases of its production.

The people at Marquand Books have done a remarkable job producing this book. In particular, special thanks go to John Hubbard for his incredible sensitivity to the work and for interpreting it with such a beautifully designed book.

Throughout the years Chinua Achebe has seen the photographs and urged me on in many ways. It is an honor to have his eloquent words accompanying them.

I am grateful to Martha Levin for believing in this project and having the imagination and courage to produce it, and to Tina Pohlman, my editor at Anchor Books, who brought it to fruition.

There are a number of friends who have seen me through this project and to whom I wish to express my deepest gratitude: Bill Arnold, Margery Aronson, Penny Auge, Adam Bartos, Robert Benjamin, Claudia Cohen, Joseph Defazio, Denzil Hurley, Elaine Mayes, Christina Roessler, Steve Reip, and Isaiah Wyner. In particular I wish to thank Jerome Liebling, whose friendship, advice, and ideas are always with me.

Finally, I am indebted to all the people in Africa whose paths I stumbled across or put myself into and who graciously and generously allowed me into their lives to photograph.

—Robert Lyons
Seattle, 1998

For Anna Lyons

An Anchor Book
Published by Doubleday
a division of Bantam Doubleday Dell Publishing Group, Inc.
1540 Broadway, New York, New York 10036

Anchor Books, Doubleday, and the portrayal of an anchor are
trademarks of Doubleday, a division of Bantam Doubleday Dell
Publishing Group Inc.

Book Design by John Hubbard
Produced by Marquand Books, Inc., Seattle
Text typeset in Walbaum, with display type in Weiss

Library of Congress Cataloging-in-Publication Data
Lyons, Robert.
  Another Africa / photographs by Robert Lyons :
 essay and poems by Chinua Achebe. — 1st ed.
   p. cm.
  ISBN 0-385-49038-0
   1. Africa—Pictorial works. I. Achebe, Chinua.
 II. Title.
 DT4.5.L96 1997
 306'.096—dc21   97-15412

ISBN 0-385-49038-0
Printed in Singapore by CS Graphics
First Anchor Books Edition: December 1998

10 9 8 7 6 5 4 3 2 1